Little
Hawaiian
Japanese
Cookbook

Muriel Miura

MUTUAL PUBLISHING

Other Cookbooks by Muriel Miura

Cookies from Hawai'i's Kitchen

Tastes and Flavors of Hawai'i

Tastes and Flavors of Pineapple

What Hawai'i Likes to Eat™

Hawai'i's Party Food

Little Hawaiian Party Food

Hawai'i Cooks with Spam®

Hawai'i Cooks and Saves

What Hawai'i Likes to Eat™ Hana Hou!

Hawai'i's Holiday Cookbook

Little Hawaiian Condiments Cookbook

Copyright © 2013
by Mutual Publishing, LLC
Recipes copyright © 2013
by Muriel Miura

All rights reserved. No part of this book may be reproduced in any form or by any electronic or mechanical means, including information storage and retrieval devices or systems, without prior written permission from the publisher, except that brief passages may be quoted for reviews.

The information contained in this book is accurate and complete to the best of our knowledge. All recipes and recommendations are made without guarantees. The author and publisher disclaim all liabilities in connection with the use of the information contained within.

This book is an abridgement of *Japanese Cooking: Hawai'i Style* (published in 2006).

ISBN: 978-1939487-24-7
Library of Congress Control Number: 2013944385

All photos © Kaz Tanabe
Illustrations © Paul Konishi

First Printing, October 2013
Second Printing, February 2016

Mutual Publishing, LLC
1215 Center Street, Suite 210
Honolulu, Hawai'i 96816
Ph: 808-732-1709
Fax: 808-734-4094
E-mail: info@mutualpublishing.com
www.mutualpublishing.com

Printed in Korea

Table of Contents

Introduction	5
Appetizers, Soup Stocks, and Soups **(Zenzai, Dashi, and Owanrui)**	
Teriyaki Meatballs (Niku No Teriyaki Dango)	8
Aku/'Ahi (Tuna) Poke (Katsuo/Maguro Butsu)	10
Sliced Raw Fish (Sashimi)	12
White Radish and Red Pepper Garnish (Some Oroshi)	14
Mustard–Soy Sauce (Karashi [Wasabi] Joyu)	14
Lemon-Flavored Soy Sauce (Lemon Joyu)	15
Delicately Flavored Soy Sauce (Tosa Joyu)	15
Spicy Dip (Chirizu)	16
Mustard or Wasabi Paste	16
Instant Soup Stock (Dashi)	17
Soybean Paste Soup (Miso Shiru)	18
Rice Dishes (Gohanmono)	
Rice Balls (Onigiri/Musubi)	21
Rice with Chicken and Egg Topping (Oyako Donburi)	24
Vinegar-Flavored Rice (Sushi)	
Basic Sushi Rice (Sushi Gohan)	27
Finger Sushi (Nigiri Sushi)	29
Tossed Sushi (Bara Sushi)	32
Hand-Rolled Sushi (Temaki Sushi)	34
Cone Sushi (Inari Sushi)	36
Noodle Dishes (Menrui)	
Noodles Cooked in Pot (Nabeyaki Udon)	40
Cold Saimin (Hiya Ramen)	42
Fried Noodles (Yaki Soba)	44

Pickled Vegetables (Tsukemono)
- Cucumber Salad (Kyuri Namasu) — 47
- Dad's Basic Vinegar Dressing (Namasu No Moto) — 49
- Pickled Yellow Turnip (Takuwan) — 50

Simmered in Sauce (Nitsuke)
- Fish Cooked in Soy Sauce (Sakana No Nitsuke) — 53
- Simmered Pumpkin (Kabocha No Fukumeni) — 54

Fried Foods (Agemono)
- Tempura Batter (Koromo) — 57
- Tempura Sauce (Tempura No Tsukejiru) — 59
- "Thorny" Tempura (Iga Age) — 60
- Aku Burger (Katsuo Dango) — 62
- Pork Cutlet (Tonkatsu) — 64
- Fried Tofu Cakes (Tofu Cakes) — 66

One Pot Cooking (Nabemono)
- Shabu Shabu with Ponzu (Shabu Shabu) — 68
- Ponzu Sauce (Ponzu) — 70
- Sesame Seed Sauce — 70
- Grated Radish Condiment (Momiji Oroshi) — 71
- Sukiyaki — 72

Broiled Foods (Yakimono)
- Basic Miso Sauce for Broiling (Miso Yaki No Moto) — 74
- Teriyaki Chicken (Matsu Kage Yaki) — 76
- Teriyaki Sauces — 78

Desserts (Dezaato)
- Baked Bean Paste Pastry (Yaki Manju) — 80
- Milk Dumplings (Chichi Dango) — 82
- Pineapple Kanten (Kanten) — 84
- Coffee–Red Bean Gelatin (Kohi-Azuki Kanten) — 85
- Japanese Doughnuts (Sata An Da Gi) — 86

Glossary — 87

Introduction

Japan has featured some of the world's most exotic, intriguing, exciting and healthy cuisine which has gained immense popularity in the Western World during the last few decades as people have become more open to experimenting with new dishes and flavors. You're invited to further explore the fascinating cookery of the Japanese in Hawai'i, with its emphasis on freshness, simplicity and elegance of presentation: the guiding principles of Japanese cooking which are followed by good cooks around the world.

Japanese cuisine always begins with the freshest ingredients. A strong sensitivity to the time of year utilizing seasonal ingredients has helped to shape a cuisine stressing dishes compatible with each season, especially in Japan. The principle of simplicity goes hand in hand with the stress upon freshness. Ingredients are prepared simply and sauced lightly to emphasize the natural flavors of ingredients. The goal of Japanese cooking is to enhance each ingredient's natural flavors and qualities.

Elegant simplicity also guides presentations in Japanese cuisine. Small portions of a few foods are gracefully and elegantly arranged on beautiful dishes in a carefully chosen composition of shapes and colors.

Many of the ingredients and cooking methods in these pages may already be familiar to you while others may not be. Nevertheless, you'll find that Japanese cooking, Hawai'i style, provides a rich source of pleasure for everyone with its more casual than the "classic" style of Japanese food preparation.

This book is a collection of some of my favorites from the days of my youth. Some of the recipes are laced with the "local touch," others feature some creative combinations of flavors, textures and colors that will add a fresh dimension to your menus. The directions for each recipe are simply written and most ingredients are available in the Asian or Oriental foods section of any market. Though each recipe has been kitchen-tested and developed to meet today's lifestyle, individual tastes differ. Use the recipes only as a guide as you use your own creativity to develop new ones.

Little Hawaiian Japanese Cooking Hawai'i Style represents the contributions of many and was published with the hope that it will contribute to the further appreciation and preservation of the legacy of the unique Hawai'i style Japanese cuisine.

Appetizers, Soup Stocks, and Soups

Zenzai, Dashi, and Owanrui

Teriyaki Meatballs
Niku No Teriyaki Dango
Yield: About 30 cocktail meatballs

1/2 pound lean ground beef
1 egg
1 tablespoon bread crumbs
2 tablespoons chopped onion
1/8 teaspoon pepper

Sauce:
1/2 cup soy sauce
1/4 cup sugar
2 tablespoons sake (rice wine)
1 teaspoon fresh grated ginger
1 clove garlic, crushed

Minced green onion, optional

Combine first 5 ingredients, mix well and shape into 3/4-inch meatballs. Place in skillet or chafing dish. Mix together ingredients for Sauce and pour over meatballs. Simmer over medium-low heat for 20 minutes. Garnish with minced green onion, if desired. Serve hot.

Aku/'Ahi (Tuna) Poke
Katsuo/Maguro Butsu
Yield: 6 to 8 servings

2 pounds aku or 'ahi fillet, cubed
1 cup ogo (seaweed), chopped
Hawaiian rock salt, to taste
1/2 teaspoon dried chili peppers, coarsely chopped
1 teaspoon sesame oil
Kukui 'inamona, to taste, optional

Combine fish with ogo, tossing gently to combine. Add remaining ingredients.

Variations:
- Season with soy sauce, minced ginger, minced green onion, red peppers, and/or thin slices of sweet onion instead of Hawaiian salt, sesame oil, and kukui 'inamona.
- Poke can be made with imitation crab, limu, abura-age (fried bean curd), king clam, or octopus instead of raw fish.

Sliced Raw Fish
Sashimi
Yield: 4 to 6 servings

1 pound fresh fillet of ʻahi, porgy, sea bass, striped bass, pink or red snapper, ulua, abalone, ʻōpakapaka, marlin, or squid
Desired garnishes (see below)
Dipping sauces (see pages 14-16)

To serve sashimi, arrange a bed of greens or garnishes on a platter; attractively arrange one or more variety of fish on the bed of greens. Place 1/2 teaspoon mustard or wasabi paste on platter for garnish; refrigerate and serve cold with dipping sauce of your choice (see pages 14-16).

Suggested garnishes for sashimi:
- Finely shredded white radish soaked in ice cold water until ready to use
- Finely shredded carrot soaked in cold water until ready to use
- Shredded lettuce
- Shredded cabbage
- Celery stalks, cut in half lengthwise, shredded, and soaked in cold water until ready to use
- Green onion curls
- Parsley
- Beefsteak plant leaves

White Radish and Red Pepper Garnish
Some Oroshi
Yield: 6 servings

1 (3-inch) piece daikon, peeled
4 dried whole red peppers
1/4 cup soy sauce
1/4 cup lemon or lime juice
1/4 cup minced green onion

Make four openings in the flat side of the daikon. Insert pepper in each opening and set aside 4 hours or overnight. Grate pepper-stuffed daikon, divide into 6 equal parts rolling each portion into a ball. Place each portion in individual serving dishes; combine with lemon juice and soy sauce; garnish with green onion to serve with sashimi.

Mustard–Soy Sauce
Karashi (Wasabi) Joyu
Yield: 6 servings.

1/4 cup soy sauce
Mustard or wasabi paste

Combine soy sauce with desired amount of mustard or wasabi paste. Serve as dip for sashimi.

Lemon-Flavored Soy Sauce
Lemon Joyu

1/4 cup soy sauce
1 tablespoon lemon juice

Combine ingredients and serve as dip for sashimi.

Delicately Flavored Soy Sauce
Tosa Joyu
Yield: 6 servings

1/4 cup soy sauce
1 tablespoon sake (rice wine)
2 tablespoons katsuobushi

Combine ingredients in saucepan; bring to a boil, stirring constantly. Strain and cool to room temperature. Pour into individual serving dishes and serve with Wasabi Paste, if desired. Serve with sashimi.

Spicy Dip
Chirizu
Yield: 6 servings

2 tablespoons sake (rice wine)
1/4 cup grated daikon
1/2 cup minced green onion
1/4 cup soy sauce
1/4 cup lemon or lime juice
1/8 teaspoon shichimi togarashi (seven pepper spice)

Heat sake in saucepan; ignite with a match and shake pan gently until flame dies out. Pour sake into small dish; cool. Combine sake with remaining ingredients. Pour into individual serving dishes and serve with sashimi.

Mustard or Wasabi Paste
Yield: 4 to 6 servings

1 tablespoon dry mustard or wasabi (horseradish powder)
1/2 teaspoon hot water

Combine to make thick paste. Set aside 5 minutes before using. Use as garnish or seasoning for sashimi.

Instant Soup Stock
Dashi

Japanese cooking has been simplified greatly with the introduction of instant dashi-no-moto. It is practical and convenient for everyday cooking, however, it can't be compared with homemade soup stock (dashi) made from shaved bonito flakes and konbu.

# cups dashi	# cups water	# teaspoons dashi-no-moto
4 cups	4 cups	2-1/2 teaspoons (1 package)
3 cups	3 cups	1-3/4 teaspoons
2 cups	2 cups	1-1/4 teaspoons
1-1/2 cups	1-1/2 cups	3/4 teaspoon
1 cup	1 cup	1/2 teaspoon

Soybean Paste Soup

Miso Shiru

Yield: 6 to 8 servings

6 cups dashi (see page 17)
6 to 8 tablespoons miso
"Tane" of choice (main ingredients, see below)
1/4 cup minced green onion

Recommended "tane" combinations:
Tofu cubes and wakame (seaweed)
Sliced bamboo shoots, wakame, and snow peas
Abura-age (fried bean curd) and satoimo (dasheen)
Tofu cubes and horenso (spinach) leaves

Bring dashi to a boil; add miso and simmer 10 to 15 minutes. Add "tane" of choice; cook additional minute or until heated through. Serve hot, garnished with green onion.

Rice Dishes
Gohanmono

Rice Balls
Onigiri/Musubi
Yield: About 10 balls

3 cups short grain rice
3-1/4 cups water

Suggested Fillings:
Umeboshi (pickled plum)
Nori tsukudani (seasoned seaweed)
Cured or smoked salmon
Dried bonito flakes mixed with soy sauce
Red pickled ginger

Suggested Coatings:
Toasted sesame seeds
Oboro (colored shrimp flakes)
Furikake (seasoned seaweed condiment)
Kinako (soybean flour) mixed with sugar
1 sheet toasted nori (laver), cut into about 5 x 2-inch strips
4 sheets sushi nori, cut each sheet into 7 strips
Salt

Wash rice; drain and add water; let stand 1 hour before cooking. To cook, place covered pot on range and cook over high heat and bring to a boil. Turn heat down to low and cook until water evaporates, about 15 minutes. Turn off heat and let stand 10 minutes before removing cover to "fluff" rice. Leave rice to cool for about 20 minutes while fillings are assembled.

To prepare the rice balls, wash hands and sprinkle a little salt onto palm of one hand; place about 1/2 cup of hot rice in hand and make a depression in center. Place about 1 teaspoon desired filling in depression; mold rice to enclose filling and shape into triangle. If desired, sprinkle with coating of your choice then wrap with a piece of nori and moisten end to seal.

Variations:
- **Spam® Musubi,** an island favorite, is made by placing a slice of canned luncheon meat, seasoned with soy sauce and sugar, on top of a rectangular mound of rice. The luncheon meat is held in place with a strip of nori.
- **Teri Chicken Musubi,** another island favorite, is made by placing a piece of teriyaki-flavored chicken on top of a rectangular mound of rice. The chicken is held in place with a strip of nori.

Rice with Chicken and Egg Topping
Oyako Donburi
Yield: 6 to 8 servings

1 pound boneless chicken, cut into thin slivers
4-1/2 cups chicken broth
6 small bamboo shoots, slivered
1 medium round onion, cut into thin slices
2 teaspoons salt
2 teaspoons sugar
2 tablespoons soy sauce
1/4 cup mirin (sweet rice wine)
1/2 cup minced green onion
6 eggs, beaten
9 cups hot cooked rice

Garnish:
Toasted ajitsuke nori

Simmer chicken in broth for 5 minutes. Add next six ingredients; bring to a boil. Add green onion. Pour beaten egg over chicken mixture. Cover and cook over low heat for 30 seconds. Serve in individual bowls over hot rice. Garnish with crushed, toasted nori (seaweed), if desired.

Variation:
- **Rice with Beef and Egg Topping (Itoko Donburi):** Substitute 1/2 pound beef cut into thin strips for chicken.

Vinegar-Flavored Rice
Sushi

Basic Sushi Rice
Sushi Gohan
Yield: 9 cups

3 cups rice
3 cups water

Vinegar Sauce (Awase-zu) No. 1:
1/2 cup rice vinegar
2 tablespoons sake or mirin (sweet rice wine)
1/2 cup sugar
1 teaspoon salt

Vinegar Sauce (Awase-zu) No. 2:
3-1/4 cups rice vinegar
1/4 cup salt
4 to 4-1/2 cups sugar
1/4 cup mirin (sweet rice wine)

Wash rice and drain. Add water and let water come to a boil; reduce heat to simmer and cook 5 to 8 minutes or until water level is reduced to level of rice. Cook additional 7 to 8 minutes over low heat. Let steam, covered, 10 minutes before transferring to large bowl or large shallow container.

Combine Vinegar Sauce ingredients; cook until sugar dissolves; cool. Sprinkle half over hot rice and toss gently. Add more Vinegar Sauce, if desired. Cool quickly. Rice is now ready to make various types of sushi.

continued on the next page

Tips:
- Use approximately 1 cup Vinegar Sauce (Awase-zu) to 5 cups cooked rice to make Sushi Rice.
- To toss rice with awase-zu, use cutting strokes sideways across the rice to avoid mashing. DO NOT MIX with circular motions. Cool quickly with a fan.
- Prepared awase-zu may be kept in sealed bottle for later use.
- Use as dressing for tossed greens or raw vegetable slices.

Finger Sushi

Nigiri Sushi

Yield: 2-1/2 to 3 dozen

Nigiri is the most famous sushi. They are hand-molded "finger-shaped" mounds of vinegared rice with slices of raw fish on top. It was developed in Tokyo as a street finger food.

4-1/2 cups Sushi Gohan (see page 27)

Suggested Toppings:
Sashimi
Cooked shrimp marinated in Vinegar Sauce for Sushi Gohan
Kamaboko
Abalone-like shellfish
Cuttlefish
Unagi (seasoned eel)

Shape rice into egg-shaped balls, slightly flattened. Dab a little mustard* or horseradish paste on top of each rice ball; press on desired topping, cut to fit size of rice ball (about 1 x 1-1/2-inch pieces). Dip in soy sauce to eat.

*Mustard: Make paste of 4 teaspoons dry mustard or wasabi with 1-1/2 teaspoons hot water; let stand 5 minutes before using.

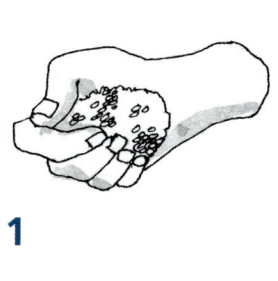

1

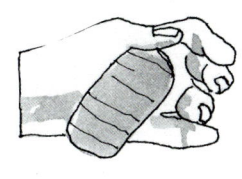

2

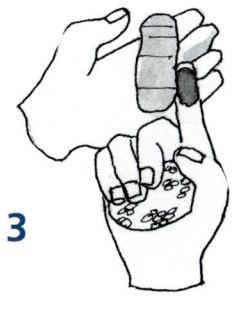

3

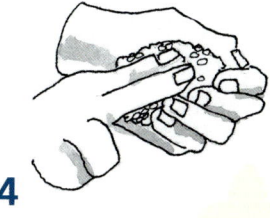

4

5

Tossed Sushi

Bara Sushi

Yield: 6 to 8 servings

1 recipe Sushi Gohan (see page 27)

Vegetables (Gu):
1 medium carrot, slivered
1 medium takenoko, slivered
1 box frozen peas
1/4 cup water or Niban Dashi
1/2 teaspoon salt
1 teaspoon sugar
2 teaspoons soy sauce
2 dried shiitake mushrooms, soaked in water and slivered

1 (4-ounce) can unagi (seasoned eel)
Fried egg strips
Ajitsuke nori strips

Combine Gu ingredients; cook 2 to 3 minutes. Drain and cool. Add to Sushi Gohan with unagi; toss gently. Garnish with fried egg strips and nori to serve.

Tip:
To prepare "Easy Bara Sushi," toss 1 (7-1/2 ounce) can Gomoku-no-tomo with Sushi Gohan and garnish as desired.

Hand-Rolled Sushi
Temaki Sushi
Yield: 12 to 15 servings

This is a fun way to enjoy sushi. Temaki means "hand-rolled" and each guest gathers together individual fillings of fish, shellfish, vegetables, and sushi rice.

9 cups Sushi Gohan (see page 27)
Nori (seaweed laver), cut into 1/2 sheets
1 avocado
1 package kaiware (white radish sprouts)
Japanese cucumber, julienned
Fresh tuna, salmon, yellowtail (hamachi) strips
King crab or imitation crab sticks
Soy sauce
Wasabi (horseradish paste)

Arrange all items attractively on platter. Place nori in palm of hand and spoon 3 tablespoons of sushi rice over and spread on nori. Place streak of wasabi along center of rice and lay desired ingredients on top. Wrap nori around filling, starting at lower end of nori and rolling into cone shape. Dip in soy sauce to eat.

Cone Sushi
Inari Sushi
Yield: 16 pieces

1 recipe Sushi Gohan (see page 27)

Vegetables (Gu):
2 shiitake mushrooms, softened and slivered
1/3 cup finely chopped carrot
1/2 cup finely chopped green beans
1/4 cup minced gobo
1 tablespoon dried shrimp
1/2 teaspoon salt
1/2 teaspoon soy sauce
1/2 cup broth or dashi (see page 17)

Fried Bean Curd Cornucopia (Abura-age):
8 triangles abura-age
2 cups rice water or plain water
2 tablespoons dried shrimp
1-1/2 cups broth or dashi (see page 17)
1 tablespoon soy sauce
1/2 teaspoon salt
3 tablespoons sugar

Combine Gu ingredients; cook 10 minutes. Drain and cool. Add to Sushi Gohan and toss gently. Fill seasoned abura-age.

Fried Bean Curd Cornucopia (Abura-age):
Cut abura-age triangles in half to make two smaller triangles. Carefully remove inner portion from each triangle. Cook in water for 30 minutes or until tender; drain, rinse, drain again. Squeeze out excess liquid.

continued on the next page

Combine remaining ingredients and simmer abura-age over low heat for 45 to 60 minutes, turning occasionally to season evenly. Drain; cool thoroughly before stuffing with Sushi Gohan mixture.

Variation:
Sprinkle "furikake" over rice; toss to mix well and stuff seasoned abura-age to make *Chirashi Inari Sushi*.

Tips:
- Asian markets have seasoned abura-age available for purchase in the refrigerator or freezer section...convenient when hosting a party or in a hurry.
- To open the abura-age without breaking them, pull apart gently from the cut end and work towards bottom. When fully open, place finger inside to open corners completely.

Noodle Dishes
Menrui

Noodles Cooked in Pot
Nabeyaki Udon
Yield: 4 servings

Dashi:
3 cups dashi (see page 17)
1/3 cup soy sauce
2 tablespoons mirin (sweet rice wine)
2 tablespoons sugar

---

1 10-ounce package cooked udon*
1/2 pound boneless chicken breast, cut into bite-size pieces
4 shrimp, cleaned and split lengthwise
1/4 cup takenoko, sliced
8 slices kamaboko
4 shiitake, softened
1 leaf hakusai (won bok or celery cabbage), cut into 1-inch pieces
2 stalks green onion, cut into 1-1/2-inch pieces
4 eggs
4 pieces Shrimp Tempura (see page 57)

Combine Dashi ingredients in a pot or divide ingredients into four parts and cook in donabe (individual ceramic hot pot); bring to a boil. Add udon and arrange remaining ingredients over udon; cover and bring to boil. Add eggs; turn heat off; cover until eggs are done, about 1 minute. Top with Shrimp Tempura to serve.

Variation:
*Spaghetti noodles may be substituted for udon.

Cold Saimin
Hiya Ramen
Yield: 4 to 6 servings

1 (9-1/2 ounce) package dried or raw saimin

Condiments (Gu):
1 small cucumber, slivered
2 cups bean sprouts, blanched
1 cup minced green onion
1 cup luncheon meat, slivered
1 cup kamaboko, slivered
1 tablespoon toasted sesame seeds

Fried egg strips
Nori strips

Dipping Sauce (Tsukejiru):
1/2 cup rice vinegar
1/2 cup soy sauce
1/2 cup sugar
1/4 teaspoon sesame seed oil
1 package dashi-no-moto
Few drops hot sauce, optional

Cook saimin as directed on package. Rinse, drain, and chill. Arrange noodles in individual serving bowls (on ice, if desired); arrange Gu over noodles.

To prepare Tsukejiru, combine ingredients in a jar; shake thoroughly. Pour over arrangement of noodles and condiments to serve.

Fried Noodles
Yaki Soba
Yield: 4 to 6 servings

1 tablespoon salad oil
1/2 cup boneless chicken or ham, slivered
1 onion, sliced
1/2 cup carrot, julienned
1/2 cup green onion, cut into 1-1/2-inch lengths
1/2 pound bean sprouts
3/4 pound fresh fried noodles or yaki soba

Seasonings:
2 teaspoons soy sauce
3 tablespoons chicken broth
1 teaspoon salt or dashi-no-moto

Garnish:
2 tablespoons toasted sesame seeds
1 tablespoon beni shoga (red ginger)
1/4 cup minced green onion or Chinese parsley

Stir-fry chicken in hot oil for 2 minutes. Add vegetables, noodles, and Seasonings; stir-fry 1 minute to heat through. Garnish with sesame seeds, beni shoga, and green onion or Chinese parsley.

Pickled Vegetables
Tsukemono

Cucumber Salad
Kyuri Namasu
Yield: 4 servings

1 cucumber
1/4 cup carrots, julienned
1/4 teaspoon salt
1/2 cup boiled clams, drained, or crabmeat
1/2 cup wakame, softened in water; cut into 1-inch pieces

1/2 cup Namasu No Moto (see next page)

Cut cucumber in half lengthwise. Slice cucumber in thin diagonal pieces; sprinkle with salt and let stand 10 to 15 minutes. Rinse salt off; drain thoroughly. Combine with carrots, clams, and wakame. Pour Namasu No Moto over and toss gently. Chill.

Dad's Basic Vinegar Dressing
Namasu No Moto
Yield: 2-1/2 cups

1 cup sugar
1 cup rice vinegar
1 tablespoon lemon zest
Juice of 1 lemon
1/2 teaspoon salt
1 tablespoon mirin (sweet rice wine), optional
1 tablespoon dried shrimp, rinsed and minced

Combine ingredients; cover and shake well. Pour over desired vegetables for namasu.

Vegetables generally used for namasu:
- Cucumber, thinly sliced
- Seaweed (ogo), cleaned and blanched
- Radishes, julienned
- Assorted greens, torn into bite-size pieces
- Bean sprouts, raw or blanched
- Beets, sliced
- Lotus root, cooked and sliced

Pickled Yellow Turnip
Takuwan
Yield: 1-1/2 pints

3/4 cup vinegar
1-1/2 cups sugar
3 tablespoons salt
1/4 teaspoon yellow food coloring
3 to 4 medium turnips, peeled
1 red pepper (optional)

Combine vinegar, sugar, and salt in saucepan. Cook over low heat until sugar and salt dissolve; cool slightly. Add yellow coloring. Slice turnip into 1/2 x 2-inch strips. Put turnips in a quart jar. Add hot liquid and pepper. Cover jar tightly. Let stand in refrigerator 1 to 2 days before serving.

Simmered in Sauce
Nitsuke

Fish Cooked in Soy Sauce
Sakana No Nitsuke
Yield: 6 servings

1/3 cup soy sauce
1/2 cup water
1 tablespoon sake (rice wine) or mirin (sweet rice wine)
3 tablespoons sugar
1/2-inch piece fresh ginger root, crushed
6 (1-1/2 to 2-pound size) whole fish, or 6 pieces fish fillet

---

Combine first 5 ingredients in large saucepan and bring to a boil. Place fish in single layer in sauce, cover, and simmer 8 to 12 minutes or until fish is cooked. Do not overcook. Serve spoonful of sauce over fish and garnish with minced green onion, if desired.

Simmered Pumpkin
Kabocha No Fukumeni
Yield: 4 to 6 servings

Simmered in a delicate sauce which enhances its fresh, natural flavor, this dish can be served either hot or cold. If your past experience with pumpkin has been limited to pies, try this new taste treat.

1-1/2 pounds kabocha (pumpkin)
2-1/2 cups dashi (see page 17)
2 tablespoons mirin (sweet rice wine)
1/3 cup sugar
1 teaspoon salt
2 teaspoons soy sauce

Cut kabocha in half, lengthwise, then cut along the groove, about 2-inches thick. Remove seeds and peel skin at 1-inch intervals, leaving strips of green.

Combine dashi with seasonings in a saucepan; bring to a boil; add kabocha. Cover and cook on medium-high heat and bring to a boil. Reduce heat and simmer for 10 to 15 minutes, or until kabocha is cooked. Turn heat off and let kabocha stand in sauce until ready to serve.

Fried Foods
Agemono

Tempura Batter
Koromo
Yield: About 2 cups batter

Koromo No. 1:
1/2 cup flour
1/2 cup cornstarch
1 egg
1/2 cup cold water

Koromo No. 2 (Puffy Tempura Batter):
1 cup flour
2 teaspoons baking powder
1 teaspoon sugar
1/2 teaspoon salt
1 egg
1/2 cup cold water
Yellow food coloring, optional

For all batters:
Sift dry ingredients together; beat egg and water together. Add liquid, all at once, to dry ingredients, mixing only until dry ingredients are moistened; batter will be lumpy. Dip seafood and vegetables into batter; deep-fry in oil heated to 365 to 375°F until delicate brown. Drain and serve hot with Tempura Sauce (see page 59).

For Lacy Tempura:
Remove 1/2 cup batter and add 2 tablespoons water for thin lacy batter. The remaining portion is the thick dipping batter. Dip fingers into think batter and sprinkle over hot oil, heated to 365 to 375°F. Repeat several times until lacy network is formed Dip prepared seafood or vegetable into thick batter and place on lacy network. When tempura is delicately brown, break network of batter to separate individual tempura; turn and fry additional minute. Drain and serve with Tempura Sauce while hot.

Some suggested ingredients for tempura are:
- Fish fillets
- Shrimps
- Asparagus spears
- Burdock root
- Sweet potato, 1/4-inch slices
- Lotus root, 1/4-inch slices
- Eggplant, 1/4-inch slices
- Ginkgo nuts on skewers
- Bell pepper, wedged
- Round onion, sliced
- Bamboo shoot, sliced

Tempura Sauce
Tempura No Tsukejiru
Yield: 4 servings

2 cups water
1 (5-inch) piece dashi konbu
1/2 cup katsuobushi (dried fish flakes)
2 teaspoons soy sauce
1/2 teaspoon salt
1/2 teaspoon sugar
1/2 cup grated turnip
1 tablespoon minced green onion

Add konbu to boiling water and cook 10 minutes. Add katsuobushi and simmer 3 minutes. Strain; add seasonings and bring to boil. Cool. Just before serving, add turnip and green onion.

"Thorny" Tempura
Iga Age
Yield: 2 dozen

1/2 pound raw seasoned fishcake, or 1 pound shrimp, cleaned
1/2 cup flour

Batter:
1 egg, slightly beaten
1/2 cup water
1/2 cup flour
1/2 cup cornstarch

4 ounces somen (Japanese noodle), broken in 3/4-inch pieces
1 quart canola oil for frying

Form fishcake into balls, about the size of walnuts. Dredge fishcake or shrimp in flour and set aside. Add egg to water and beat to combine; add to dry mixture and stir until ingredients are blended together.

Dip fishcake balls or shrimp in batter; roll in somen. Deep-fry in oil heated to 365°F, until golden brown. Drain on absorbent paper and serve hot.

Aku Burger
Katsuo Dango
Yield: About 12 patties

1-1/2 pounds aku
1 block tofu, wrapped in dish cloth with water squeezed out thoroughly
3 tablespoons minced round onion
3 tablespoons minced green onion
1/4 cup gobo (burdock), skin scraped off, rinsed, and shaved into fine slivers with sharp knife; soak in water until ready to use; drain water thoroughly
1/2 teaspoon grated fresh ginger
1 teaspoon soy sauce
1 large egg, beaten
Salt and pepper to taste

Canola oil for frying

Using wide, large cutting board cut aku into small pieces then mince. Combine all ingredients except oil in large mixing bowl and mix well with hand. Divide into about four portions, and return each portion to the cutting board and chop with cleaver until well blended. Form into small patties and fry in hot oil until golden brown. Drain on absorbent paper. Serve hot with steamed rice. Sprinkle soy sauce over, if desired.

Pork Cutlet
Tonkatsu
Yield: 3 to 4 servings

1 pound lean pork, cut into 1/2-inch-thick slices
1/2 teaspoon salt
1 egg, slightly beaten
1-1/2 cups cornflake crumbs, dry bread crumbs, or "panko"

1 quart canola oil for frying

Sauce:
1/2 cup catsup
3 tablespoons Worcestershire sauce
Dash of pepper

Salt pork and dip in beaten egg. Dredge in panko, cornflake or dry bread crumbs, and fry in oil heated to 365°F for 2 to 3 minutes or until golden brown. Drain on absorbent paper. Mix Sauce ingredients and blend thoroughly. Spoon sauce over cutlets to serve.

Variation:
- **Chicken Cutlet (Tori Katsu):** Substitute boneless chicken breast cutlets for pork.

Fried Tofu Cakes
Tofu Cakes
Yield: About 2-1/2 dozen pieces

1 block tofu
1/4 cup cooked shrimp, chopped
1/2 cup minced carrot
1/3 cup green beans, chopped
1/4 cup finely chopped roasted peanuts
1/3 cup gobo (burdock root), finely chopped
2 tablespoons sugar
1-1/2 teaspoons salt
3 eggs, beaten

1 quart canola oil for frying

Press out excess water from tofu; strain through sieve. Place in large bowl and add remaining ingredients; mix thoroughly. Drop mixture by spoonfuls into oil heated to 365°F. Fry until golden brown; drain on absorbent paper. Best served hot.

One Pot Cooking
Nabemono

Shabu Shabu with Ponzu

Shabu Shabu

Yield: About 4 to 6 servings

A great party dish that has gotten its name from the sound made by swishing the ingredients back and forth in the boiling broth.

1-1/2 pounds top sirloin, cut into paper-thin slices
6 cups chicken or beef broth or dashi (see page 17)
1 (4-inch) piece dashi konbu
1 bunch watercress, cut into 1-1/2-inch lengths
1 medium round onion, sliced
12 stems green onion, cut into 1-1/2-inch lengths
1 box frozen broccoli spears, cut into 1-1/2-inch lengths, optional
1/2 pound cooked udon (noodles)

Ponzu Sauce (see page 70)
Sesame Seed Sauce (see page 70)
Momiji Oroshi (see page 71)

Condiment:
Chopped green onion

Arrange beef, vegetables, and noodles attractively on a platter and place on dining table. Combine ingredients for Ponzu Sauce and pour into four small dishes and set before diners. Bring broth to boil. Add konbu and remove after 1 minute. Dip beef in the boiling broth until it turns a light pink. Cook vegetables in the same manner. Add the noodles last, cooking only until reheated. Each guest cooks a choice of meat or vegetables in the broth. Dip into Ponzu or Sesame Sauce with desired condiments to eat.

Note: The broth may be served as the last course, if desired. Any combination of your favorite vegetables may also be used.

Ponzu Sauce

Ponzu

Yield: 4 servings

1 cup soy sauce
1 cup green onion, finely chopped
1/4 cup rice vinegar
1/4 teaspoon hot sauce
Momiji Oroshi (see page 71)

Combine ingredients for Ponzu Sauce and pour into four small dishes and set before diners. Use for Shabu Shabu on page 68.

Sesame Seed Sauce

Yield: 4 servings

1/2 cup white sesame seeds, toasted and ground
3 tablespoons dashi (see page 17)
2 tablespoons rice vinegar
1-1/2 tablespoons soy sauce
1 tablespoon mirin (sweet rice wine)
1/4 teaspoon monosodium glutamate

Combine ingredients for Sesame Sauce. Use for Shabu Shabu on page 68.

Grated Radish Condiment
Momiji Oroshi

1/2 pound white radish (daikon)
2 or 3 red chili peppers, seeded

Condiments:
1 cup green onion, finely chopped
Momiji Oroshi
Grated turnip
Red pepper, seeded and minced

Peel daikon. Pierce holes in end of daikon and stuff with red pepper, then grate. Liquid is gently squeezed out. Or, add red pepper powder to grated daikon.

Sukiyaki

Yield: About 4 servings

Sauce:
2-1/2 cups soy sauce
1-1/2 cups sugar
1/2 cup mirin (sweet rice wine)

Sukiyaki:
1/4 cup chicken or beef broth
1 cup onion, sliced
1 pound beef or chicken, thinly sliced
1 cup bamboo shoots, sliced
1/2 block tofu, cubed
1/2 cup mushrooms, sliced
1/2 bunch long rice, softened in water and cut into 4-inch lengths
2 cups watercress, washed and cut into 1-1/2-inch lengths
1 cup green onion, cut into 1-1/2 inch lengths

Combine Sukiyaki Sauce ingredients and broth in large skillet; arrange onion, beef or chicken, bamboo shoots, tofu, mushrooms, and long rice attractively in sauce. Cook over medium-high heat 3 to 4 minutes, spooning sauce over ingredients as they are cooking. Just before serving, add watercress and green onion. Serve with hot rice.

Broiled Foods
Yakimono

Basic Miso Sauce for Broiling

Miso Yaki No Moto

Yield: 4 to 6 servings

1-1/2 pounds fish fillet or top round steak, cut into serving pieces

Miso Sauce:
1-1/2 cups miso
3/4 cup sugar
1 to 2 tablespoons mirin
1/2 teaspoon grated fresh gingerroot

Combine Miso Sauce ingredients. Marinate fish or beef slices in Miso Sauce overnight. If whole fish is used, cut slashes on each side of fish and salt lightly. Stuff fish cavity with Miso Sauce; fry or broil.

Broil fish or beef slices on outdoor grill over medium to high heat for 3 to 5 minutes on each side or until of desired doneness.

Teriyaki Chicken
Matsu Kage Yaki

Yield: 2 to 4 servings

4 pieces boneless chicken breast*
1/4 cup Basic Teriyaki Sauce (see page 78)
1 tablespoon toasted sesame seeds, optional

Marinate chicken pieces in Teriyaki Sauce for 30 minutes. Broil on outdoor grill over low or medium heat, skin side up on grid. Baste frequently and turn; cook 10 to 15 minutes or until done.

*Whole broiler or frying chicken may be used. Cook over low or medium heat on outdoor grill for 40 to 60 minutes or until done. Wrap in foil, if desired.

Variation:
- **Broiled Teriyaki Catfish (Namazu No Kabayaki):** Substitute 1 pound catfish for chicken.

Teriyaki Sauces

Yield: About 3 to 4 cups

Teriyaki Sauce #1:
2 cups soy sauce
1/2 cup sake or mirin (sweet rice wine)
2 cups sugar
1 clove garlic, crushed
1-1/2 teaspoons grated fresh gingerroot

Teriyaki Sauce #2:
2 cups soy sauce
1/2 cup sake or mirin
1 cup brown sugar, packed
1 clove garlic, crushed
1 teaspoon grated fresh gingerroot

Combine ingredients in jar; cover and shake until well blended. Use as marinade for beef, pork, poultry, fish, shellfish, and lamb.

Desserts
Dezaato

Baked Bean Paste Pastry
Yaki Manju
Yield: 2 dozen

Dough:
2-1/2 cups flour
1 tablespoon sugar
1/2 teaspoon salt
1 cup salad oil
6 tablespoons cold water

---

1 cup prepared canned koshi or tsubushi an (bean paste)

Combine flour, salt, and sugar; blend thoroughly. Add oil and water to dry ingredients and mix thoroughly. Shape dough into small rounds, using approximately one tablespoon dough. Flatten dough to form circles. Place a generous teaspoonful of an (bean paste) or filling of choice in the center of each circle and pinch edges together to seal. Place seam side down on ungreased cookie sheet. Bake at 400°F for 30 to 35 minutes or until golden brown.

Variations:
- Use 2 (10-ounce) cans refrigerated buttermilk biscuits instead of mixing own dough.
- Use canned apple, peach, or pineapple pieces instead of an for filling.

Milk Dumplings
Chichi Dango
Yield: About 5 dozen

2/3 cup water
2/3 cup evaporated milk
1 (10-ounce) package mochiko (rice flour)

Syrup:
1-1/4 cups sugar
1/4 cup water

Few drops red or green food coloring, optional

Combine first three ingredients and mix well. Wrap in double thickness of cheesecloth and steam 30 to 35 minutes.

Combine Syrup ingredients and bring to a boil; cool. Pour over steamed mixture placed in a bowl, a little at a time, blending well. Place in cake pan sprinkled with katakuri (potato) starch; cool. Cut into desired shapes and sizes; roll in mochiko and wrap individually.

Variation:
- **Soybean Powder Dumplings (Kinako Mochi):** Dredge dumplings in kinako before serving or wrapping individually.

Pineapple Kanten

Kanten

Yield: 32 (1 x 2-inch) pieces

2 sticks white kanten
3-1/2 cups water
1/2 cup pineapple juice
1 cup sugar
1/4 teaspoon lemon extract
1 cup crushed pineapple, drained
Drop of yellow food coloring

Wash kanten, tear into small pieces, and soak in water for 30 minutes. Add sugar; cook until sugar and kanten dissolve, stirring occasionally. Add coloring; strain into 8-inch square pan. Cool and chill until it congeals. Cut into desired shapes to serve.

Coffee–Red Bean Gelatin

Kohi-Azuki Kanten

Yield: 12 to 16 pieces

1/4 cup (4 envelopes) unflavored gelatin
1/2 cup cold strong coffee
2-1/2 cups hot coffee
1 can sweetened condensed milk
1 can tsubushi an
Dash of salt, optional

Sprinkle gelatin over cold coffee; let stand 15 to 20 minutes. Combine hot coffee with condensed milk and tsubushi an (bean paste); mix well. Add softened gelatin to hot mixture and stir until gelatin dissolves. Pour into 8 x 8-inch pan and refrigerate until firm. Cut into desired sizes to serve.

Japanese Doughnuts
Sata An Da Gi
Yield: 2-1/2 to 3 dozen

3 cups flour
1 cup sugar
4-1/2 teaspoons baking powder
1/2 teaspoon salt
3 eggs, slightly beaten
1/4 teaspoon vanilla, optional
1 cup milk

1 quart salad oil for deep-frying

Sift dry ingredients together. Combine eggs, vanilla, and milk; beat well and add to dry ingredients. Mix thoroughly. Drop by teaspoonfuls into oil heated to 375°F. Cook about 2 minutes or until golden brown. Drain on paper towel, and roll in sugar, if desired.

Glossary

A

Abura-age: Fried bean curd
Agemono: Fried foods
'Ahi: Hawaiian name for yellowfin tuna
Ajitsuke nori: Seasoned dried laver; seaweed
An: Sweetened red bean paste
Awase zu: Seasoned vinegar
Azuki: Small red beans

B

Beni shoga: Pickled red ginger

D

Daikon: White Japanese radish
Dango: Dumpling, meatball, or croquette
Dashi: Basic broth; basis of all Japanese soups; used in cooking numerous dishes
Dashi-no-moto: Japanese instant soup stock granules
Dashi konbu: Kelp used for soup stock

E

Edamame: Soybeans

F

Furikake nori: Japanese seasoned seaweed mix

G

Gobo: Burdock root
Gohan: Cooked rice
Goma: Sesame seeds
Gu: Ingredients

H

Hakusai: Chinese cabbage

I

Ika: Squid, cuttlefish
Inari sushi: Sushi rice stuffed in a cone-shaped fired tofu

K

Kamaboko: Steamed fish cake
Kanten: Agar agar
Karashi: Dry mustard
Katakuri: Potato starch
Katsuobushi: Dried bonito (tuna) flakes
Kinako: Soybean flour
Konbu: Dried seaweed; kelp
Koromo: Batter
Koshi an: Strained red bean paste

M

Maguro: Japanese name for tuna
Manju: Bean paste-filled bun
Matsutake: Mushroom
Menrui: Noodles
Mirin: Sweet Japanese rice wine
Miso: Fermented Japanese soybean paste
Mochiko: Rice flour

Momiji oroshi: Grated turnip with red chili pepper

N

Nabemono: One-pot dishes
Namasu: Vinegar-flavored Japanese vegetable dish
Niku (gyuniku): Beef
Nitsuke: Simmered in soy sauce and sugar
Nori: Dried laver; seaweed

O

Oboro: Dried shredded shrimps
Ogo: Japanese term for seaweed
'Ōpakapaka: Pink snapper

P

Panko: Japanese style bread crumbs
Ponzu: Mixture of soy sauce and citrus juice

R

Ramen: Saimin; noodles

S

Sakana: Fish
Sake: Japanese rice wine
Sashimi: Raw fish
Satoimo: Dasheen taro
Shichimi togarashi: Seven flavors spice; blend of pepper leaf, poppy seed, rape seed, hemp seed, dried tangerine peel, and sesame seed
Shiitake: Dried mushrooms
Shiso: Beefsteak plant
Shoyu: Japanese term for soy sauce; seasoning made from roasted corn and steamed soybeans mixed with malt-mold, salt, and water, then fermented.
Soba: Buckwheat noodles
Somen: Fine noodles made from wheat flour
Su: Rice vinegar
Sushi: Vinegar-flavored rice

T

Takenoko: Bamboo shoot
Takuwan: Pickled turnips
Tare: Dipping sauce
Tempura: Fritters
Teriyaki: Soy-flavored sauce; grilling food while basting with teriyaki sauce
Tofu: Soybean curd or cake
Togarashi: Red chili pepper
Tsubushi an: Coarsely mashed red bean paste
Tsukemono: Pickled vegetables

U

Udon: Thick noodles made of wheat flour
Ulua: Hawaiian name for trevally/crevalle
Umeboshi: Red pickled plum
Unagi: Freshwater eel

W

Wakame: Lobe leaf; dried seaweed
Wasabi: Green horseradish powder

Y

Yaki manju: Baked pastry with red bean filling
Yakimono: Grilled foods